THIS BOOKS BELONGS TO:

Rhianna Walker

24/4/22

Printed in Great Britain
by Amazon

79486209R00068